THE TEACHINGS OF ZOROASTER

AND THE PHILOSOPHY OF THE PARSI RELIGION

SHAPORJI ASPANIARJI KAPADIA

CONTENTS

EDITORIAL NOTE	1
AUTHOR'S PREFACE	2
INTRODUCTION	4
EXTRACTS	27
NOTES	53

EDITORIAL NOTE

THE object of the editors of this series is a very definite one. They desire above all things that, in their humble way, these books shall be the ambassadors of good-will and understanding between East and West, the old world of Thought, and the new of Action. In this endeavour, and in their own sphere, they are but followers of the highest example in the land. They are confident that a deeper knowledge of the great ideals and lofty philosophy of Oriental thought may help to a revival of that true spirit of Charity which neither despises nor fears the nations of another creed and colour. Finally, in thanking press and public for the very cordial reception given to the "Wisdom of the East" series, they wish to state that no pains have been spared to secure the best specialists for the treatment of the various subjects at hand.

L. CR R-BYNG.
S. A. KAPADIA.
The Orient Press,
4, Harcourt Buildings,
Inner Temple, London.

AUTHOR'S PREFACE

ZOROASTRIANISM is a religion much commented upon by a few enthusiastic oriental scholars, and less understood by the general public. Out of the millions of believers of this faith in the bygone ages, there now remains a handful of devout followers, known as the Parsis. I have, therefore, ventured to put before my readers a brief sketch of the teachings of this divine prophet. I hope, that the strangers to the faith may find in it food for philosophic enlightenment, and the Zoroastrians themselves a subject for deeper and wider researches in the untold wealth of sublime theology and philosophy, now looked up in the monumental tomes of the ancient Avesta writings.

For extracts in this volume, I am greatly indebted, amongst others, to the works of the following eminent oriental scholars: Dr. Martin Haug, Dr. E. W. West, Dr. L. H. Mills, Professors Max Müller, Spiegel, Bleeck, Westergaard, Z. A. Ragozin, J. Darmesteter, Mr. K. R. Cama, *Ervard* Kavasji Edalji Kanga, Mr. N. M. N. Kanga, Mr. J. A. Pope, and Dr. J. Adams.

I have also to thank the India Office authorities for their kindness in placing at my disposal their splendid library of the Persian and Zend literature, and my old friend Sir C. Purdon Clarke, the Director of the Victoria and Albert Museum, South Kensington, for his valuable suggestions regarding the ancient print of Zoroaster, which appears on the cover of this book, and my friend Mr. A. Kapadia, of Lincoln's Inn, for his kind assistance.

S. A. KAPADIA.
Inner Temple, London,
January 1*st*, 1905.

INTRODUCTION

"I WILL now tell you who are assembled here the wise sayings of Mazda,[1] the praises of Ahura,[2] and the hymns of the Good Spirit, the sublime truth which I see rising out of these flames. You shall therefore hearken to the Soul of Nature. Contemplate the beams of fire with a most pious mind! Every one, both men and women, ought today to choose his Dread. Ye offspring of renowned ancestors, awake to agree with us." So preached Zoroaster, the prophet of the Parsis, in one of his earliest sermons nearly 3,500 years ago.

Imbued from his infancy with deep philosophical and religious thoughts for the welfare and well-being of mankind, this ancient prophet of Bactria derived his holy inspiration after thirty years of divine meditation on a secluded and inaccessible mountain-top of "Ushidarena." Thus fortified in communion with Ahura-Mazda, "Spitama Zarathustra" proceeded to the city of Balkh, at the time the capital of the King of Iran, Kava Vishtaçpa. [3]

Clothed in pure white flowing vestments, bearing with him the sacred fire, [4] "Adar Burzin Mehr," and a staff or sceptre made of a cypress tree, this sage of antiquity appeared before the court of Kava Vishtaçpa. By persuasion and argument he unfolded his religious mission; and proclaimed the mandate of Ahura, in order to elevate the ancient faith of the Aryas to its lofty and intellectual purity of monotheism.

Somewhere in the region washed by the eastern shires of the Caspian Sea, on the fertile soil of Atropatene, the primeval Aryas toiled and laboured in peaceful pastoral pursuit. In the early days of

Zoroaster homage was paid and prayers were offered to the Supreme Being, usually through the recognized symbols of the Deity. The heavenly firmament, tinted with cerulean hue—one limitless vault of refulgence and indescribable splendour—the resplendent orb of the rising sun, the ethereal gentleness of the beaming moon, with her coruscating companions, the planets and the stars, the verdant earth, the swift-flowing river, murmuring in sweet cadence of eternity and bliss, the roaring sea of life and death, and the glorious fire of Empyrean,—all these, in the days of the primitive Aryan religion, were believed to be so many manifestations of the Almighty God, and were accordingly symbolized. Things, which were originally manifestations of God's good work, became in course of time personified; assumed shapes of deities in the frail imagination of the devotees; and finally came to be adored in lieu of the Great Architect of the world. Thus, a religious system, in itself philosophically sublime, degenerated into a system of polytheism, having for its object adoration of idols and visible forms of good and evil spirits, reflective of human imagination. This was the great evil, the crime of ignoring the Creator for the created, which our prophet Zarathustra laboured to remedy; and to restore the then ancient faith to its pristine purity of Ahura worship was his chief object.

This led to a schism amongst the Indo-Eranians. One branch of the ancient Aryas, powerfully supported by the State, became Mazdayasnians (Monotheists), and the other of the same stock remained staunch to the worship of material gods, and were known as Daêvayasnians (Polytheists). Inevitable war of creed and faith resulted in the migration of the weaker and polytheistic branch to the fertile plains of India, where it took root and blossomed into the absolute Brahminism of the modern Hindoos. The other remained on the native soil, flourished for centuries, built up an empire, and finally in its turn gave place to the Moslem hordes of Arabia. It migrated, and by the irony of Fate, sought and obtained shelter with religious toleration among the banished sister branch of the primeval stock.

The appearance of Zoroaster, to teach his excellent religion before King Gushtasp and his wise and learned courtiers, may be well compared to that of St. Augustine before King Ethelbert in the sixth century of the Christian era. It is a curious historical coincidence that in both oases extreme piety, religious convictions, eloquent and persuasive arguments, prevailed. England received the blessings of Christianity through the Saxon King Ethelbert, and rose in its might to be a great Christian nation, whose empire in the twentieth century of the Christian era extends over land beyond the seas; and under whose sceptre are folded together vast millions of most loyal subjects of His Britannic Majesty King Edward VII. So, 3,500 years ago, did the mighty Gushtasp of Iran espouse the cause of Zoroaster and spread the Mazdayasnian religion to all the corners of his vast empire. He was the first founder of the doctrine of the State religion. Under the renowned and mighty warriors Cyrus and Darius of Persia, the national flag of State and Zoroastrianism, welded together in unity, proudly floated over untold millions, who claimed protection and paid homage to the Persian Court. Thus, through generations and generations, flourished Zoroastrianism, to be ultimately shattered and almost annihilated by the Arabs of the Khaliph Omar at the battle of Nehâvand, A.D. 642. Subsequent events may well be described in the words of Thomas Moore:

> *"Is Iran's pride then gone for ever,*
> *Quenched with the flame in Mithra's caves?*
> *No-she has sons, that never—never*
> *Will stoop to be the Moslem's slaves,*
> *While heaven has light or earth has graves."*

Inspired with zealous fervour, conquered but never vanquished, a few Magian fathers of the East boldly sallied forth in a frail bark to seek their fortunes in other climes. After undergoing terrible hardships, they floated, at the mercy of the tempestuous ocean, to the hospitable shores of Western India. Since then, centuries have passed, and the Parsis have made themselves known in the West for their charity and benevolence; for their staunch loyalty to the Crown; for their commercial, educational, and political achievements.

I have often wondered what powerful. influence, what intrinsic philosophy, what imperceptible charm of thought and theology have been at work to endear Zoroastrianism to the heart of the modern Parsis—devoid as it is of the powerful support of the State; uprooted from its native soil and transplanted for centuries amongst the Hindoos. In the following pages I shall endeavour to show why

Zoroastrianism has maintained its divine power and prestige amongst them.

Nearly 3,500 years ago, at Rae, in Media, there lived a man of the name of Pourushaspa, who led a holy and righteous life with his wife Dogdho.

It is related of this holy man, on the authority of the ninth chapter of the Yaçna, that, being desirous of perpetuating his posterity, he prepared a religious ceremony as a thanksgiving to the Almighty, and solemnly prayed for the favour of a child. This worthy man's prayers were duly answered, and a son was born to him, who laboured amongst our primitive forefathers for the amelioration of mankind and their deliverance from the everlasting ruin. His mission was prior to the advent of Buddhism, Christianity, and Islam.

He left behind him, written in letters of golden fire, in the History of the World, his illustrious name, Zarathustra, as a permanent landmark and everlasting beacon for the welfare of the body and the guidance of the soul in its passage from the known to the unknown.

"O Maker of the material world! to what greatness, goodness, and fairness, can this daêva-destroying teaching [Monotheism] of Zoroaster be compared?"

The answer came:

"As high as Heaven is above the earth, which it encompasses, so high above all other utterances the law of Mazdeism stands."[5]

> "You shall therefore hearken to
> the Soul of Nature"

I shall now explain the theology and moral philosophy of the religion of Zoroaster. It is purely a monotheistic religion, based on the worship and adoration of *Ahura-Mazda*, the "All-knowing Lord." It teaches:

(1) Of the life on the earth:
(2) Of the life hereafter:
(3) Of Immortality of the soul and the resurrection of the body.

Briefly, it teaches and develops the noblest instinct of mankind —*viz.*, as Zoroaster himself has termed it, "The Soul of Nature." In the word-picture of the solemn chants of the Gathas of the Zoroastrian religion, a notion of God of all the Universe is convincingly interwoven.

He, to whom no form, shape, or colour is attributed, stands alone, *Omni Unique*, the Nature of Infinite of *Infinite Perfection*. It is not given to mortals of finite mind to define Him, the most just, the most benevolent, the most merciful. He is One, who dwells in boundless space, clothed in the most resplendent and illumined glory of inscrutable Nature. In Khordah-Avesta, the prayer-book of the Parsis, God describes all His attributes, in the following words:

"I am the Keeper; I am the Creator and the Maintainer; I am the Discerner; I am the Most Beneficent Spirit.

"My name is the Bestower of Health; the Priest; Ahura [the Lord]; Mazda [the All-knowing]; the Holy; the Glorious; the Farseeing; the Protector; the Well-wisher; the Creator; the Producer of Prosperity; the King who rules at His Will; One who does not deceive; He who is not deceived; He who destroys malice; He who conquers everything; He who has shaped everything; All Weal; Full Weal; Master of Weal; He who can benefit at His wish; the Beneficent One; the Energetic One; Holiness; the Great One; the Best of Sovereigns; the Wise One."[6]

"He is the Light and Source of Light; He is the Wisdom and Intellect. He is in possession of all good things, spiritual and worldly, such as good mind [*vohumano*], immortality [*ameretad*], health [*haurvatad*], the best truth [*asha vahista*], devotion and piety [*armaiti*], and abundance of every earthly good [*Khshathra vairya*]. All these gifts He grants to the righteous man who is upright in thoughts, words, and deeds. As the ruler of the whole universe, He not only rewards the good, but He is a punisher of the wicked at the same time." [7]

In the Zoroastrian Liturgy (Yaçna I.), Zarathustra describes God as

(1) "The Creator Ahura-Mazda, the Brilliant, Majestic, Greatest, Best, Most Beautiful.

. . . . .

(4) "who created us, who formed us, who keeps us, the Holiest among the heavenly."[8]

The scope of this work does not permit me to discuss comparative theology; but this I will say, that ancient as the Zoroastrian religion is, no more comprehensive, lucid, and intelligible definition of the Great Creative Cause can be found in any religious books of the modern religions. It is worthy of note that Milton, who wrote nearly

2,500 years after Zoroaster, had grasped the true spirit of the Zoroastrian ideal of God.

> *"Unspeakable who sit'st above these heavens,*
> *To us invisible or dimly seen*
> *In these Thy lowest works, yet these declare*
> *Thy goodness beyond thought, and power divine."*

. . . . . .

Having established the belief in the Great Creative Power, Zoroaster proceeded to strengthen and fortify his followers by carefully warning them against the influence of the Evil Spirit. One of the greatest evils in the time of the prophet was the tendency of the populace to adore and worship God's manifestations or created elements. Slowly, superstitious belief, for want of good guidance, created imaginary and fanciful gods, who were materialized in idols, and worshipped at the whim of the believer. In the language of the period, amongst the ancient Aryas, the word *Daêva* signified God, from the Aryan root *div*, to shine, and consequently all those personified manifestations of Nature were called *Daêvas*. Zoroaster quickly perceived that the ancient monotheistic religion of the Aryas was degenerating into a state of image and idol worship. He had already taught the people "The Soul of Nature." It became necessary that he should stamp out the so-called *idol-daêvas*.

Thenceforth Zoroaster, in the Avesta language, used the word *Daêva* in the sense of an evil or wicked spirit. The old root *div*, to shine, has given us such words as *Deus* in Latin, *Daêva* in Sanskrit, *Zeus* in Greek, and *Tius* in German, for God. The Avesta language of Zoroaster is the only ancient language in which quite a contrary and evil meaning is attached to this word, and, so far as this religion is concerned, the word *daêva* still has an evil meaning. Had the great Xerxes been successful in his wars with the Greeks, the Mazdayasnian faith would have been established in the West, and all the modern languages would probably have been now using the word *Daêva* for the Devil, or the Evil One.

Let me but for a moment lift the veil, and show you the most hallowed and impressive picture of Zoroastrian speculative philosophy. In the plenitude of the creation there, one perceives the hand of the Creator in His Mighty Majesty, creating and completing this universe at six different periods—first, the heavenly firmament; second, water; third, the earth; fourth, plants; fifth, lower animals; and sixth and last, man. Man is created free to act after his own heart and understanding.

"I have made every land dear to its dwellers, even though it had no charms whatever in it,"[9] said Ahura-Mazda to Zoroaster.

Sixteen different regions and countries created by Ahura-Mazda are carefully described in the first Fargard of the Vendidad, giving a more or less geographical notion to modern readers of the origin of the population in Central Asia.

But the most important speculative philosophy, disclosed by this Fargard, is the existence of two primeval Causes in the state of Nature, working in opposition to each other, known in the Avesta language as *Spenta Mainyus* (the Creative or Augmenting Spirit), and *Angro Mainyus* (the Destructive or Decreasing Spirit). Since the creation, there has been an incessant state of conflict between these rivals; the records of these encounters, in which man as a free agent plays his part with his soul for a stake, are bound up in the annals of the world, to be finally unfolded, read and adjudged on the great Day of Judgment.

This philosophy of the Good and the Evil Spirit, creative of the material world, is not to be confused with the idea of dualism. Many learned writers, of European fame, have clearly proved that Zoroaster did not preach dualism. The Evil Spirit is not endowed with any of the attributes of the Almighty; neither is he placed in opposition to, or made a rival of, God. I have carefully read the exhaustive comments made by Western scholars on this subject, some in favour, and the majority of them against the theory of dualism.

As a great deal of controversy has been raised on the doctrine of two rival spirits, I think it necessary to quote from the Avesta, and also from the later Pahlavi text, to prove that dualism is not one of the doctrines preached by Zoroaster.

"Ahura-Mazda, through omniscience, knew that Ahriman exists. . . .

"The Evil Spirit, on account of backward knowledge, was not aware of the existence of Ahura-Mazda. . . .

"He [Ahura-Mazda] sets the vault into which the Evil Spirit fled, in that metal; he brings the land of hell back for the enlargement of the world, the renovation arises in the universe by his will, and the world is immortal for ever and everlasting. . . .

. . . So it is declared that Ahura-Mazda is supreme in omniscience and goodness, and UNRIVALLED in splendour.

Revelation is the explanation of both spirits together: one is he who is independent of unlimited time, because Ahura-Mazda and the region, religion, and time of Ahura-Mazda were and are and ever will be; while Ahriman in darkness, with backward understanding and desire for destruction, was in the abyss, and it is he who *will not be*."

Amongst others, the celebrated Dr. West, to whom the Parsis are greatly indebted for his researches in the Avesta writings, finally refutes the charge of dualism brought against Zoroastrianism by some learned divines, who discovered dualism through the spectacles of modern religions.

"The reader will search in vain for any confirmation of the foreign notion that Mazda-worship is decidedly more dualistic than Christianity is usually shown to be by orthodox writers, or for any allusion to the descent of the good and evil spirits from a personification of 'boundless time' as asserted by strangers to the faith."[10]

Reading carefully Fargard I. of the Vendidad, I cannot help admiring the sublime theory of Nature, so far as it relates to the Destructive Spirit. Now, what are the evils employed by Angro Mainyus? A great serpent; winter months freezing water and earth, and retarding the growth of fruit-bearing trees and other vegetation useful to mankind; a poisonous wasp; evil thoughts; wild beasts destructive to animal kind; doubt or unbelief in the Creator; indolence and poverty; idol and image worship; devastation or plague; sorcery; fevers; falsehood; darkness; noxious smells; and wickedness.

These are the few evils employed by Angro Mainyus to retard the progress of, and if possible, destroy mankind. It is quite evident, that the sole aim of Zoroaster's teachings is to raise God's best and fairest work—man—to that level of human perfection by good words, good thoughts, and good deeds, so as to enlist the services of the Good Spirit. Spenta Mainyus being thus invoked, a protection from evils can be obtained; and the soul of man at the trumpet-call can be clothed in a fit and proper state of piety to render homage to his Creator.

Of the Life on the Earth

A graphic description of sixteen of the regions and countries created by the Almighty is given in the Vendidad. They extend from the shores of the Caspian to the banks of the Indus in Hindustan. The favoured man of God was *Yima*, known in the Shah Nameh as Jamshid. To him God's command, "Enlarge My world, make My world fruitful, obey Me as Protector, Nourisher, and Overseer of the World," was given. Yima was presented with a plough and a golden spear, as symbols of sovereignty. He set to work to carry out this holy mandate, brought large tracts of land into cultivation and filled them with men, cattle, beasts of burden, dogs, birds, and ruddy burning fires.

Imagination soars high at this picture of pastoral bliss, of peaceful occupation in cultivating the virgin soil and propagating the species. Evil was unknown. The day of perpetual brightness, the summer of radiant joy, and all heavenly peace had cast their mantle of transcendent glory over the land of Iran, of which Yima was God's chosen overseer.

Little did Yima know that there existed in the state of Nature the Evil Spirit (Angro Mainyus), to attempt to mar his handiwork by snow, frost, and deluge.

"He [Evil Spirit] does not think, nor speak, nor act for the welfare of the creatures of Ahura-Mazda; and his business is unmercifulness and the destruction of this welfare, so that the creatures which Ahura-Mazda shall increase he will destroy; and his eyesight [evil eye] does not refrain from doing the creatures harm."

Yima, by his piety and devotion to the Creator, had enlisted the services of the Good Spirit, and through him it was made manifest to him that on this corporeal world snow, frost, and deluge would come. He was warned of this disaster in time, and ordered to prepare an enclosure large enough to hold cattle, beasts of burden, useful animals, men and women, of the largest, best, and most beautiful kinds, together with birds, red burning fires, and seeds of all kinds of trees—"all these in pairs"—without any blemish or tokens of the Evil Spirit (Angro Mainyus).

Pious Yima, like Noah of old, benefited by this timely counsel, and ultimately succeeded in saving the chosen creation, which formed his ancient domain of Airyana-Vaêjâ.

One cannot help noting in the Zoroastrian Scriptures a certain similarity to the later-day history of Noah and his ark. Spenta Mainyus planted the seed of a good fruit-bearing tree, nourished it with water of purity, cultivated it with honest industry and diligence, watched its growth in divine contemplation of its blossoming forth good thoughts, good words, and good deeds (*humata*, *hukhta*, and *havarahta*), when from "the region of the North . . . forth rushed Angro Mainyus, the deadly, the Daêva of the Daêvas," and with one chill blast of snow and frost ("Falsehood" and "Wickedness," *vide* Avesta) smote and retarded the rising sap of the growing tree. Thus, high from above, war was declared between Good and Evil, between the Pious and the Wicked, between Light and Darkness,—one preserving and the other smiting God's glorified works.

A good portion of the Zoroastrian theology is directed towards protecting mankind in his efforts to fight against Angro Mainyus and his wicked accomplices.

"That one wish which Ahura-Mazda, the Lord, contemplates, as regards men, is this, that 'Ye shall fully understand Me; for every one who fully understands Me, comes after Me and strives for My satisfaction.'"[11]

Zoroaster, in order to stem the tide of destruction, went to the root of the evil and laid the foundation-stone of his great moral philosophy, by making certain well-defined hygienic rules and regulations to preserve the pastoral community from being totally destroyed by pestilence, which we know as a visitation of God. In this brief sketch I shall enumerate a few of them for the appreciation and due consideration of my readers.

Putrefaction or decomposition, occasioned by the dead bodies, from which thousands of untold evils may arise, was the first subject dealt with in the sacred books of the Avesta. It is written, that directly death occurs, the evil element of putrefaction, known in the Avesta language as "Drukhs Naçus," takes possession of the dead body. In the figurative language of the period, "Drukhs Naçus" (putrefaction) is personified into a pernicious fly, full of filth and disease, and capable of spreading great harm among the living creation. The duration of the period at which it takes possession of the dead body greatly depends on the nature and the cause of death. Modern medical science has nearly elucidated this mystery of cadaverous rigidity and the exact time of the putrefaction of the body. These have been graphically described in Fargard VII. of the Vendidad.

Careful instructions are given as to the part of the house, and the manner, in which the dead body should be kept, pending its ultimate disposal; the place of its final rest, where it may dissolve into its natural elements; the subsequent purification of the place where the body may have lain in the house; the people who carry the corpse; the clothes that may have come in contact with it; and the purification of the flowing water in which the corpse may have been found.

"Purity is the best thing for men after birth," says the Avesta. Those who are desirous of further investigating the subject will be handsomely repaid their trouble in perusing Fargards V., VI., VII., VIII., and IX. of the Vendidad, wherein they will find scientific instructions as to the germ theory and the preservation of the public health. Though enunciated thousands of years ago, they are now carefully and minutely followed by western nations in the twentieth century.

Next in order comes the command to cultivate the soil, to produce corn, provender, and fruit-bearing trees, to irrigate dry land and drain the marshes, and to populate the whole with men, cattle, and useful beasts of burden. Zoroastrian philosophy shudders with horror at the contemplation of the motherly earth being defiled by the burial therein of dead bodies, and consequently means are devised of disposing of corpses on high mountain tops by birds of prey or by the process of nature. The modern Parsis, in accordance with the ancient regulations, have devised Towers of Silence. The Parsis of Bombay are grateful to their ancient prophet, who taught them the great hygienic principle of sanitation.

During recent years it has saved them, a handful as they are, from the bubonic plague. This great "Drukhs Naçus" carried away thousands of natives, hour by hour and day by day, and yet signally failed in his wholesale attack on the Parsis. The reason is obvious. The armour of health, forged by Zoroaster during his pious contemplation of thirty years' duration on the mount "Ushidarena," and so fittingly worn by the Parsis of the present day, is invulnerable to the attack of Angro Mainyus and such of his satellites as "Drukhs Naçus." Strict ordinances are made for the care and welfare of women during certain periods, including those of gestation and child-birth, so that no injury may happen in the latter instance to the parent and the offspring and to those who have to assist at this great function of Nature.

Besides these, there are numerous directions as to observing cleanliness in ordinary daily life, all tending to the care and purification of the body and prevention of infectious diseases by contact.

"This is purity, O Zarathustra, the Mazdayasnian law.

"He who keeps himself pure by good thoughts, words, and works.

"As to the right purity of one's own body, that is the purification of every one in this corporeal world for his own state,

"When he keeps himself pure by good thoughts, words, and works."[12]

Having made men invulnerable to diseases, Zoroaster proceeded to look after their morals. His moral philosophy deals with two attributes inherent in man the Good Mind and the Evil Mind. These two are allegorically termed "Vohumana" (the Good Mind) and "Akamana" (the Evil Mind).

Thoughts, words, and deeds are liable to the influence of either "Vohumana" (the Good Mind) or "Akamana" (the Evil Mind). Zoroaster has summed up the whole of his moral philosophy in three expressive words—"Humata" (good thoughts), "Hukhta" (good words), and "Hvarshta" (good deeds). The way to heaven is laid through these three mystic avenues, and the seeker of them is borne through with the self-consciousness of having spent his allotted span of life to the use and furtherance of God's good creation, and to His eternal glory.

"Turn yourself, not away from three best things—Good Thought, Good Word, and Good Deed."

By "Good Thoughts," a Zoroastrian is able to concentrate his mind in divine contemplation of the Creator, and live in peace, unity, and harmony with his fellow-brethren. For the love of his fellowmen, he is enjoined to protect them in danger; to help them in need and want; to raise their understanding in education; to enable them to enter into holy bonds of matrimony; and to the best of his resources to enhance the prosperity and welfare of the community of his brotherhood in particular, and of all mankind in general.

By "Good Words," he is enjoined not to break his contract with others, to observe honesty and integrity in all commercial transactions, faithfully to pay back any borrowed money at the risk of being called a thief, to prevent hurting the feelings of others, and to engender feelings of love and charity in the Mazdayasnian fraternity.

By "Good Deeds," he is directed to relieve the poor, deserving and undeserving, to irrigate and cultivate the soil, to provide food and fresh water in places where needed, to encourage matrimony, and to devote the surplus of his wealth in charity to the well-being and prosperity of his co-religionists and others.

The Parsis of India are too well known for their disinterested charities amongst the people of all denominations to need any eulogistic remarks from me. It is a matter of great pride to me, as a Parsi, and a subject of deep thankfulness to God, as one of His beings, that in this matter my co-religionists in the East have truly and faithfully, and with the utmost tolerance, distributed their wealth in wise and useful charities, to lessen the sorrows and untold miseries, and brighten the homes of our less fortunate brethren.

"I praise the well-thought sentiment, the well-spoken speech, the well-performed action.

"I praise the good Mazdayasnian law, the free from doubt, removing strife." [13]

One can picture to himself the properly ordained household of a Zoroastrian, who has carefully imbibed the abstract principles of "Humata," "Hukhta," and "Hvarshta," and put them to practical purposes in an ordinary workaday life.

Marriage is particularly recommended as a great factor towards leading a religious and virtuous life, in addition to the social comforts of physical, mental, and moral recreations. The household of a man 6f well-regulated mind is his peaceful domain, wherein he is the lord with his worthy consort, both entwined together and actuated by that religious affinity which the Zoroastrian religion, by wise and philosophical precepts, never fails to infuse. As the land improves by fertilization, so should mankind by union, says the Zoroastrian philosophy. One of the five things most pleasing to God, mentioned in Fargard III. of the Vendidad, is that a holy man should build himself a habitation, provide himself with a wife, children, fire, and a herd of cattle. The husband is required to obey the laws of health and be brave, to protect and preserve his family from any outside violence, to be industrious, to provide them with necessaries of life, to be tolerant, truthful, and chaste, and to complete the domestic happiness of his family circle.

Chastity and implicit obedience from a wife to her husband are considered to be the greatest virtues in a woman, the breach whereof will be punished as a sin.

In every way, the wife is equal to her husband in social status, enjoying perfect liberty of action. These wise domestic regulations are so faithfully followed by the modern Parsis that misbehaviour or misconduct of a woman is altogether conspicuous by its absence. Divorce for misconduct is almost an unknown thing, and the writer cannot but congratulate his community on the fact of total absence of women of loose morals.

It is one of the ordinances of the faith that a father must look after the spiritual and temporal education of his children, and bring them up well fortified physically and morally to fight the battle of life with perseverance, diligence, honesty, and integrity, thus enhancing the reputation of his family and the honour of his community.

"May the desirable obedience come hither, for joy to the men and women of Zarathustra." [14]

Tolerance is another great feature of the Parsi faith. Though taught to revere his own religion and despise and destroy idols and images, he is also impressed with the idea of observing great tolerance and discretion in passing judgment on the religious belief of others. Zoroaster himself set the example of this excellent precept, whilst praising the soul ("Fravashi").

"The Fravashis of the pure men in all regions praise we." [15]

It is evident that he prayed for all wise and holy men and women who believed in God. That the same spirit exists to the present day, is proved by the munificent gifts of the Parsis for charitable purposes to people, irrespective of creed or caste, having for their sole object the relief of mankind.

Strict as the law of chastity is, a great spirit of tolerance is shown in the Avesta writing in reference to an unmarried woman, who happens to fall a victim to the charms of an insidious man. True, it is a punishable sin, yet the Almighty, in His mercy, has taken due notice of such a misfortune happening in a household.

In the poetic language of the Avesta, it is laid down that a virgin, who whilst under the protection of her parents, either betrothed or not betrothed, is in a way to become a mother, should not for the very shame of the act attempt to destroy herself. She must not add to the sin already committed, a further and more heinous crime of self-destruction. Further, she is forbidden, under the penalty of a grave sin, from seeking to destroy the fruit of her body, either with the assistance of her partner in the guilt or that of her parents in order to hide her shame from the world. She must not seek, at the instigation of her betrayer from the path of chastity, the assistance of "an old woman" versed in herbology. The putative father must protect the unfortunate partner of his guilt and the child.

Here is a tragic drama of the twentieth century, so often enacted in our criminal courts, written and commented upon by Zoroaster in his gospel, in the primitive pastoral age, at the beginning of the history of the world. What thoughts, what deep moral philosophy, what superhuman knowledge, must have been invoked by the great

Iranian sage to soften the hardships of life, by introducing a ray of heavenly mercy, of which Tom Hood sang centuries after:

> *"Take her up tenderly*
> *Lift her with care;*
> *Fashion'd so slenderly,*
> *Young and so fair.*
>
> *"Touch her not scornfully;*
> *Think of her mournfully,*
> *Gently and humanly;*
> *Not of the stains of her—*
> *All that remains of her*
> *Now is pure womanly."*

The whole creation is placed under the guardianship of God as the head, and six Ameshaspends (archangels). Ameshaspends are mystical guardian spirits, who work night and day incessantly for the welfare and protection of the creation committed to their charge by the Almighty.

God is the protector of man.

(1) Bahman is given the custody of all useful domestic animals and birds.

(2) Ardibihist has the control of fire and life-giving heat.

(3) Shahrevar is the president of all kinds of metals and minerals.

(4) Aspandarmat is the custodian of the earth, with injunctions to keep it fruitful, clean, and cultivated.

(5) Khordat has to see to the purity of water and water-courses.

(6) Amerdad tends to trees and vegetation.

With the assistance of Yazats (angels) night and day they police this earth and guard their respective charges against the encroachment of the Evil Spirit (Angro Mainyus).

Zoroaster, having dealt with the welfare of mankind, has not forgotten lower animals in his moral philosophy. Special regulations are laid down for their kind and considerate treatment. He has recognized the necessity of slaughtering animals for human food, prescribed which kinds of animals and birds are fit for that purpose, and shown the most humane and expeditious methods of killing them methods which, curiously enough, are now recommended and adopted in this country by public authorities. Unnecessary slaughter is forbidden, and shooting for mere pleasure is absolutely discountenanced.

One instance, woven in traditional Oriental imagery, will suffice to convey the sentiments of the Parsis on this subject. The Over-Lord of the herd of the domestic cattle (Geush-Urvan) raises his plaintive call of heart-rending pathos to the Almighty Creator, and humbly beseeches His intercession to alleviate the pain and sufferings his fellow-kind have to undergo at the hand of men. The poor petitioner becomes aware of the fact, that in accordance with the pre-arranged plan, his herd was created for the support and advancement of the corporeal world; that it is expected of them to furnish flesh food and milk, and to be useful to the cultivator of the soil. In return men are enjoined, under penalty of severe punishment, to be kind and attentive to their many wants, and merciful in their necessary slaughter. The bovine leader is further informed that Zoroaster, by sweetness of speech, will assuage their sufferings and engender a benevolent spirit of humanity amongst their cruel tormentors. The dumb petitioner, whose vision of protection being limited to the sole aspiration of obtaining the support of a powerfully armed warrior, is not able to understand that in many instances persuasive and convincing words are far more potent than a sharp-edged sword of the best tempered steel and more effective in their purpose than the brute force of a salient blow.

As to kindness to dumb animals, the following passage from Patet Erani [16] (Khordah-Avesta) will show what the Zoroastrians think:

"Of all kinds of sins which I have committed with reference to Heaven against the Ameshaspend Bahman [the protector of cattle] with reference to the world against the cattle and the various kinds of cattle, if I have beaten it, tortured it, slain it wrongfully, if I have not given it fodder and water at the right time, if I have castrated it, not protected it from the robber, the wolf, and the waylayer, if I have not protected it from extreme heat and cold, if I have killed cattle of useful strength, working cattle, war-horses, rams, goats, cocks, and hens, so that alike these good things and their protector Bahman have been injured by me and not contented with me, I repent."

This merciful and ancient teaching does not call for the intervention of any public society to prevent cruelty to animals, so far as the Parsis are concerned. I humbly venture to suggest, that it is not the imposition of fine or imprisonment by the Civil Law of the country that deters the evil-doer. What is wanted, is a sound doctrine of moral philosophy, as expounded by Zoroaster, preached and brought home to these people by a carefully organised system. Man has conscience and a soul to be saved; and, however hardened his nature may have become, it is within the bounds of possibility to awaken him to his wickedness and cowardice to dumb animals, who patiently and courageously work for him, and are the means of procuring him ease and comfort in his worldly existence.

Unlike other religions, it condemns fasting or total abstaining from food as a wicked and a foolish act, which injures and enervates the body.

"No one who does not eat, has strength to do works of holiness, strength to do works of husbandry. By eating, every material creature lives; by not eating, it dies away." [17]

"With us the keeping of fast is this, that we keep fast from committing sin with our eyes, and tongue, and ears, and hands, and feet. . . .

"Since I have spoken in this manner, and have brought forward the fasting of the seven members of the body, that which, in other religions, is fasting owing to not eating, is, in our religion, fasting owing to not committing sin [excess]."[18]

Readers, such are a few salient principles of the Zoroastrian theology of the Life on the Earth, which I now close by quoting from the Vendidad:

> "Increase, live the whole Time of thy Life,
> as long as thou wilt live." [19]

"Of the Life Hereafter"

"Yet know, vain sceptics! know, th' Almighty Mind,
Who breathed on man a portion of His fire
Bade his free soul, by earth nor time confined,

To heaven, to immortality aspire."

Slowly and solemnly, now I approach this subject of great theological mystery, of the migration from the known to the unknown universe.

". . . The worldly existence is, in the end, death, and disappearance, and of the spiritual existence, in the end, that of a soul of the righteous is undecaying, immortal, and undisturbed, full of glory and full of enjoyment, for ever and everlasting, with the angels and archangels and the guardian spirits of the righteous."

The hour of departure rings out in solemn silence, when the severance of terrestrial friendship and unity which existed in him as a man must take place—one to ascend, and the remnant to dissolve into its elements. The scriptures of Zoroaster most vividly describe this solemn event, and give evidence right through of the great belief in immortality of the soul and the resurrection of the body.

At the glorious sunset of the pious life, the soul remains three days near his lifelong friend the body, and perceives and "sees as much joyfulness as the whole living world possesses." For him, the fourth day dawns in *gloria in excelsis*. From the midst of his worldly nearest and dearest relatives, friends, and neighbours, the soul, having been bidden pious adieux in holy blessings, ascends in the company of his guardian angel, Shros, to render his account at the gate of "Chinvat Bridge." In his upward ethereal journey, floating in the region of the sweet-scented balm of the south soft wind, he meets his own astral self, transformed into a handsome figure of gracefulness and seraphic beauty. This figure reveals itself to him as his Good Thoughts, Good Words, and Good Deeds. Pleased with his welcome, and having rendered his account to Mehr Davar, the recorder at the gate of Heaven, he passes the barrier to eternal bliss and happiness, and awaits his body on the great day of resurrection. On the contrary, there is a drastic picture drawn of the soul of a wicked man. It must suffer till the last day of the Great Gathering, when everybody will be judged, the battle will end, the Evil Spirit will no more have power to play man as a pawn, and there will be everlasting peace—peace and happiness. The subject is a vast one, and the space limited for this purpose does not permit me, as I should like, to deal with it *in extenso*. I hope the extracts given on this subject will interest the readers.

A sinful soul need never despair of mercy and forgiveness of God. Wicked as he may have been, a due notice of any good deed done by him will be taken into consideration by the Great Merciful. One of the numerous questions asked by Zoroaster of Ahura-Mazda, was in reference to a man whose body was feeling the torments of hell, with the exception of his right foot. It was participating in the heavenly bliss and comfort. The man was a wicked king in the world below, who ruled his country with oppression, lawlessness, and violence. He was incapable of practising any known virtue. One day, when he was out hunting for his pleasure, he saw a goat, tethered to a stake, vainly trying to reach a morsel of hay. The sight of a poor hungry beast straining at the rope kindled a spark of mercy in his otherwise obdurate heart. Thus moved by a sudden impulse, he, with his right foot, kicked the morsel of hay within reach of the famished beast. The incident was duly recorded in the Book of Fate, and the foot received its reward. This legend, savouring of antiquity, and backed up by ancient authorities, reveals to a Zoroastrian the sublime doctrine of reward and punishment.

After a youth has attained the age of fifteen and sought the Zoroastrian Law, he is enjoined to be liberal in thoughts and deeds, pious, and religious in ceremonial rites, just and wise as a ruler, truthful and honest in his dealings, careful in keeping the elements pure and undefiled, active in destroying evil, attentive to the care and want of the domestic animals, industrious in cultivating and irrigating land, persevering in education of himself and others, temperate in all desires, and useful to mankind in promoting harmony, concord, and unity amongst his kinsfolk, friends, and others. He must carefully weigh the merits and demerits of every step he has to take on the path of life. If by want of knowledge or ignorance, he does anything which turns out to be a sinful act, he must, at the earliest possible opportunity, rectify and remedy the same. From his early youth he is taught the belief that all his good and evil deeds will be duly recorded; that with the flight of time they will grow, multiply, and accumulate. On the day of the ascension of his soul, the recording angel Mehr Davar will ask him to render an account of his short span of corporeal life, before bidding him enter that place of supreme bliss, known to the modern Parsis as "Garothman Behest."

Readers of this brief sketch might say that this is a philosophy *couleur de rose*. Nay, ask yourselves the question, What has been achieved by the teachings of Zoroaster? You will find that they have brought peace and happiness to Parsi households; they have made them loyal and peace-abiding subjects of the British Crown, and a benevolent community to the people of the world; they have lessened pauperism, crime, infamy, and immorality; they have made them a race worthy of its proud traditions, which command the respect, confidence, and admiration of those with whom they come in contact. It is very rare to find a Parsi of a criminal instinct. Crime mania, if it can be designated as such, has no suitable soil prepared for it to flourish in, in a Parsi community. It must wither in its very inception, for the antidote prepared by Zoroaster, and faithfully handed down from generation to generation to his disciples and followers, has raised an effective rampart against the approach of this foul and degrading instinct.

At the moment of writing this, a subject of vast importance to my fellow-creatures in this country passes in review before me. In the course of my professional duties I have been, on numerous occasions, an unwilling spectator of many tragic dramas which are daily enacted in our criminal Courts. Within a few yards of gaiety and pleasure, prosperity and brilliancy, one can easily step into a veritable slum life of this great metropolis, A poor, half-starved, pale, and delicate-looking waif, bootless and hatless, with scarcely a semblance of garments, spies your intrusion into his domain. It is sad to contemplate his fate, his end, and his ultimate destination. This fruit, of ill-conditioned parents, grows up to look upon society as his natural foes to be preyed upon. Hardened and rendered callous by the rigour of the criminal law, the nation has in him an utterly worthless and a dangerous man. One asks, Has he heard a word of moral truth? Has he been taught the moral philosophy? Has he acquired the conception of God and Nature? Thoughtless, friendless, homeless, and Godless, he roams, a prey to the Evil Mind (Akamana). In the next scene of life we find him the willing slave of the devil (Angro Mainyus). One step further and a sentence from the black-capped judge, is his reward; a short delay, and then comes the end. Who can tell the terrible anguish, the torturing thoughts, and the painful agonies of unrestrained remorse of this wretched being, who is awakened and enlightened at the eleventh hour by the ministration of some holy man of God? Sad to say, it is too late for this earth. Standing on the threshold of eternity for one brief moment, listening to the soothing words of his own burial service, he mutely prays what? For God's forgiveness for those who could have done better for him and his wretched kind. Let me ring down the curtain in mercy to one more miserable soul that has gone aloft to render his account.

It is not the fault of one class of men or the other; it is not the fault of the clergy that God's superior and gifted animal has been allowed to become a prey of the Evil Spirit and then hounded out of existence by our law: it is the fault of our system, want of unity, of proper charitable organisation, and of discriminate support by the well-to-do and prosperous class. Were Zoroaster to visit this country, I venture to say, that his first step in practical moral philosophy would be to organize a national institution, where these poor waifs and strays could be bent from their infancy to the righteous path of Good Thoughts, Good Words, and Good Deeds.

Then the nation will be rewarded by the sight of the sons of the soil, marching in distant climes for the glory and honour of the British flag, as soldiers of God and the King, and pioneers of the ever-extending British Empire, as did their heroic brethren in Persia of old under the victorious flag of illustrious Gāo. [20]

Resurrection

I cannot do better than refer to the following passage in "Bundahis," on this subject.

Zarathustra asked Ahura-Mazda, "Whence does a body form again which the wind has carried and the water conveyed; and how does the resurrection occur?"

Ahura-Mazda answered thus: "when through Me the sky arose from the substance of the ruby, without columns, on the spiritual support of far-compassed light; when through Me the earth arose, which bore the material life, and there is no maintainer of the worldly creation but it; when by Me the sun and moon and stars are conducted in the firmament of luminous bodies; when by Me corn was created so that, scattered about in the earth, it grew again and returned with increase; when by Me colour of various kinds was created in plants; when by Me fire [21] was created in plants and other things without combustion; when by Me a son was created and fashioned in the womb of a mother, and the structure severally of the skin, nails, blood, feet, eyes, ears, and other things was produced; when by Me legs [22] were created for the water, so that it flows away, and the cloud was created which carries the water of the world and rains there where it has a purpose; when by Me the air was created which conveys in one's eyesight, through the strength of the wind, the lowermost upwards, according to its will, and one is not able to grasp it with the hand outstretched; each one of them, when created by Me, was herein more difficult than causing the resurrection, for it is an assistance to Me in the resurrection that they exist, but when they were formed it was not forming the future out of the past."

According to the ancient "Bundahis," [23] at the time of the resurrection, the soul will demand its original body out of the custody of the three known elements the Earth, the Water, and the Fire. All the dead will rise with consciousness of their good and evil deeds. At the Great Assembly, in the presence of the righteous, they will penitently deplore their misdeeds. Then will there be the separation of the righteous from the wicked for three nights and days the wicked,

> *"Full in the sight of Paradise,*
> *Beholding Heaven and feeling Hell."* [24]

The reign of terror, at the end of the stipulated time, vanishes into oblivion, and its chief factor Ahriman goes to meet his doom of total extinction, whilst Ahura-Mazda the Omnipotent Victor remains the Great All in All.

After this great penance, God in His mercy prepares a bath of purification, through which all pass, and arise in sanctified purity. Hallowed and conscious of all ties of relationship and friendship which existed in their terrestrial life, they glide, in company with the hierarchy of Heaven, into the domain of Immortality for ever and everlasting.

The memory of the dead is handed down, from generation to generation, in religious ceremonies, which are periodically performed by the priests. One incident I must mention before closing this sublime theme. On an occasion somewhat similar to the Christian "All Souls" Day, the souls of the Zoroastrians visit this sublunary earth once a year. Those, who have participated in the ceremonies on these occasions, can but feel that heavenly inspiration which becomes one's nature by faith and strict pious devotion. During the period of this pious visit, every Parsi household is thoroughly cleansed of the minutest impurity. In the best room of the house, a place is set apart, full of choice sweet-scented and fragrant flowers, and fruits—a perfect picture of peaceful bliss—with fire of sandal-wood burning, and the priests and members of the household, in the midst of a glorious illumination, chanting hymns of glory to God and His creation, Let there be no dissent from a picture so nobly grand and a ceremony so sublime, as it is but an innocent homage to God's infinite blessings, and to us a source of comfort to hold communion with and feel in spirit the presence of those whom we have loved, respected, and adored—fathers and mothers, wives, brothers and sisters, relations and friends—who have done their duty and have gone before us, in accordance with the law, and with whom we hope to mingle—the body, dust to dust, the soul, in eternal bliss of "Garodemana." [25]

S. A. KAPADIA.
Inner Temple, London,
January 1905.

---

1. All-Knowing.
2. The Lord
3. King Gushtasp.
4. Symbol of Life.
5. Free translation of Fargard V. of the Vendidad.
6. Ormuzd Yast. Tr. by Darmesteter.
7. Dr. Haug.
8. For further information on this subject see extracts Yaçna XLIV.
9. Fargard I. of the Vendidad.
10. Dr. E. W. West's "Introduction to the Sacred Books of the East," Vol. 18.
11. Dinâ-î Maînôg-î Khirad.
12. Fargard X. of the Vendidad.
13. Yaçna XIV.
14. Yaçna LIII.
15. Farvardin-Yasht.
16. A prayer of repentance for sin.
17. Fargard III. of the Vendidad (Darmesteter).
18. Sad Dar LXXXIII.
19. Fargard XVIII. (Bleeck's Translation).
20. See notes.
21. Means life or vitality.
22. Conduit, canal or water ways.
23. "Original Creation" (a book).
24. "Lalla Rookh" (Thomas Moore).
25. "House of hymns"—the highest Heaven.

EXTRACTS

PURITY [1]

"Purity is for man, next to life, the greatest good that purity is procured by the law of Mazda to him who cleanses his own self with Good Thoughts, Words, and Deeds.

"Make thyself pure, O righteous man! Any one in the world here below can win purity for himself, namely, when he cleanses himself with Good Thoughts, Good Words, and Good Deeds."

PRAYER OF ASHEM-VOHU [2]
FROM KHORDAH-AVESTA

1. "Purity is the best good.
2. "Happiness, happiness is to him:
3. "Namely, to the most pure in purity."

THE LAW OF AHURA-MAZDA [3]

". . . The law of Mazda cleanses the faithful from every evil thought, word, and deed, as a swift-rushing, mighty wind cleanses the plain.

. . . . .

"So let all deeds thou doest be henceforth good. . . . A full atonement for thy sin is effected by means of the law of Mazda."

COMMANDMENTS FOR THE BODY AND THE SOUL [4]

The sage asked the Spirit of Wisdom thus: "How is it possible to seek maintenance and prosperity of the body without injury of the soul, and the preservation of the soul without injury of the body?"

The Spirit of Wisdom answered thus: "Him who is less than thee consider as an equal, and an equal as a superior, and a greater than him as a chieftain, and a chieftain as a ruler. And among rulers one is to be acquiescent, obedient, and true-speaking; and among accusers be submissive, mild, and kindly regardful.

"Commit no slander; so that infamy and wickedness may not happen unto thee. For it is said that slander is more grievous than witchcraft.

. . . . .

"Form no covetous desire, so that the demon of greediness may not deceive thee, and the treasure of the world may not be tasteless to thee.

"Indulge in no wrathfulness, for a man when he indulges in wrath becomes then forgetful of his duty and good works . . . and sin and crime of every kind occur unto his mind, and until the subsiding of the wrath he is said to be just like Ahareman. [5]

"Suffer no anxiety, for he who is a sufferer of anxiety becomes regardless of enjoyment of the world and the spirit, and contraction happens to his body and soul.

"Commit no lustfulness, so that harm and regret may not reach thee from thine own actions.

"Bear no improper envy, so that thy life may not become tasteless.

. . . . .

"Practice no sloth, so that the duty and good work, which it is necessary for thee to do, may not remain undone.

"Choose a wife who is of character, because that one is good who in the end is more respected.

. . . . .

"Thou shouldst be DILIGENT and MODERATE, and EAT OF THINE OWN REGULAR INDUSTRY, and provide the share of the sacred beings and the good; and thus the practice of this in thy occupation is the greatest good work.

. . . . .

"With enemies fight with equity. With a friend proceed with the approval of friends. With a malicious man carry on no conflict, and do not molest him in any way whatever. With a greedy man thou shouldst not be a partner, and do not trust him with the leadership.

With an ill-famed man form no connection. With an ignorant man thou shouldst not become a confederate and associate. With a foolish man make no dispute. With a drunken man do not walk on the road. From an ill-natured man take no loan.

. . . . .

"In forming a store of good works thou shouldst be diligent, so that it may come to thy assistance among the spirits.

"Thou shouldst not become presumptuous through any happiness of the world; for the happiness of the world is such-like as a (aloud that comes on a rainy day, which one does not ward off by any hill,

"Thou shouldst not become presumptuous through much treasure and wealth; for in the end it is necessary for thee to leave all.

. . . . .

"Thou shouldst not become presumptuous through great connections and race; for in the end thy trust is on thine own deeds.

"Thou shouldst not become presumptuous through life; for death comes upon thee at last, and the perishable part falls to the ground."

THE SOUL'S DESTINATION[6]

1. Zarathustra asked Ahura-Mazda: "Ahura-Mazda, Heavenly, Holiest, Creator of the corporeal world, Pure! when a pure man dies, where does his soul dwell during this night?"

2. Then answered Ahura-Mazda: "Near his head it sits itself down, reciting the Gâthâ Ustavaiti, praying happiness for itself: 'Happiness be to the man who conduces to the happiness of each. May Ahura-Mazda create, ruling after His wish.' On this night the soul sees as much joyfulness as the whole living world possesses."

3. "Where does the soul dwell throughout the second night?"

4. Then answered Ahura-Mazda: "Near his head it sits itself," etc. (as in verse 2).

5. "Where does his soul stay throughout the third night?"

6. Then answered Ahura-Mazda: "Near his head it sits itself," etc. (as in verse 2).

7. "When the lapse of the third night turns itself to light, then the soul of the pure man goes forward, recollecting itself at the perfume of plants. A wind blows to meet it from the mid-day region, a sweet-scented one, more sweet-scented than the other winds.

. . . . .

9. "In that wind there comes to meet him his own law in the

figure of a maiden, one beautiful, shining, with shining arms; one powerful, well-grown, slender, with large breasts, praiseworthy body; one noble, with brilliant face, one of fifteen years, as fair in her growth as the fairest creatures.

10. "Then to her (the maiden) speaks the soul of the pure man, asking: 'What maiden art thou whom I have seen here as the fairest of maidens in body?'

11. "Then replies to him his own law: 'I am, O youth, thy good thoughts, words, and works, thy good law, thine own law of thine own body—which would be in reference to thee like in greatness, goodness, and beauty, sweet-smelling, victorious, harmless, as thou appearest to me.

12. "Thou art like me, O well-speaking, well-thinking, well-acting youth, devoted to the good law, so in greatness, goodness, and beauty as I appear to thee.

. . . . .

14. "'Thou hast made the pleasant yet more pleasant to me, the fair yet fairer, the desirable yet more desirable, that sitting in a high place, sitting in a yet higher place, in these Paradises Humata, Hûkhta, Hvarsta (Paradises) . . . .

15. "'The soul of the pure man goes the first step and arrives in (the Paradise) Humata; the soul of the pure man takes the second step and arrives at (the Paradise) Hûkhta; it goes the third step and arrives at (the Paradise) Hvarsta; the soul of the pure man takes the fourth step and arrives at the Eternal Lights.'"

. . . . .

19. Zarathustra asked Ahura-Mazda: "Ahura-Mazda, Heavenly, Holiest, Creator of the corporeal world, Pure! when a wicked one dies, where does the soul dwell throughout this night?"

20. Then answered Ahura-Mazda, "There, O pure Zarathustra, near the head it runs about whilst it utters the prayer Ké mánm, etc., 'Which land shall I praise, whither shall I go praying, O Ahura-Mazda?' In this night the soul sees as much displeasing as the whole living world.

25. "When the lapse of the third night approaches towards light, O pure Zarathustra, then goes the soul of the wicked man to the impure place, recollecting itself continually by the stench. To it comes a wind blowing from the North Region, an evil-smelling one, more evil-smelling than other winds.

26. "When the soul of the wicked man receives this wind into

the nose, it goes (saying), 'Whence comes this wind which I smell with the nose as the most evil-smelling wind?'

. . . . .

33. "The fourth step takes the soul of the wicked man and it arrives at the darknesses without beginning."

THE SOUL'S RENDERING OF ACCOUNT [7]

"The thirteenth question is that which you ask thus: Who should prepare the account of the soul as to sin and good works, and in what place should they make it up? And when punishment is inflicted by them, where is their place then?

"The reply is this, that the account about the doers of actions, as to good works and sin, three times every day whilst the doer of the actions is living, Vohûmano the archangel should prepare; because taking account of the thoughts, words, and deeds of all material existences is among his duties.

"And about the sin which affects accusers, which is committed by breakers of promises, even in the world Mitrô is said to be over the bodies, words, and fortunes of the promise-breakers; and as to the amount, and also as to being more than the stipulation when there is a period of time, Mitrô is the account-keeper. In the three nights' account Srôsh the righteous and Rashnû the just are over the estimate of the limits of the good works and sin of righteousness and wickedness. In the future existence, on the completion of every account, the Creator Aûharmazd Himself takes account, by whom both the former account of the three nights and all the thoughts, words, and deeds of the creatures are known through His omniscient wisdom.

"The punishment for a soul of the sinners comes from that spirit with whom the sin, which was committed by it, is connected; fostered by the iniquity practised, that punishment comes upon the souls of the sinful and wicked, first on earth, afterwards in hell, and lastly at the organisation of the future existence. When the punishment of the three nights is undergone the soul of the righteous attains to Heaven and the best existence, and the soul of the wicked to hell and the worst existence. When they have undergone their punishment at the renovation of the universe they attain, by complete purification. from every sin, unto the everlasting progress, happy progress, and perfect progress of the best and undisturbed existence."

GATHA HYMN[8]

"This I ask Thee, O Ahura! tell me aright: when praise is to be offered, how shall I complete the praise of the One like You, O Mazda? Let the One like Thee declare it earnestly to the friend who is such as I, thus through Thy Righteousness within us to offer friendly help to us, so that the One like Thee may draw near us through Thy Good Mind within the soul.

"This I ask Thee, O Ahura! tell me aright: how, in pleasing Him, may we serve the Supreme One of the better world?

. . . . .

"This I ask Thee, O Ahura! tell me aright: who by generation was the first father of the Righteous Order? Who gave the recurring sun and stars their undeviating way? Who established that whereby the moon waxes, and whereby she wanes, save Thee? These things, O Great Creator! would I know, and others likewise still.

"This I ask Thee, O Ahura! tell me aright: who from beneath hath sustained the earth and the clouds above that they do not fall? Who made the waters and the plants? Who to the wind has yoked on the storm-clouds, the swift and fleetest too? Who, O Great Creator! is the inspirer of the good thoughts within our souls?

"This I ask Thee, O Ahura! tell me aright: who, as a skilful artisan, hath made the lights and the darkness? Who, as thus skilful, hath made sleep and the zest of waking hours? Who spread the Auroras, the noontides and midnight, monitors to discerning man, duties, true guides?

"This I ask Thee, O Ahura! tell me aright these things which I shall speak forth, if they are truly thus. Doth the Piety (which we cherish) in reality increase the sacred orderliness within our actions? To these Thy true saints hath she given the Realm through the Good Mind. For whom hast Thou made the Mother-kine, the producer of joy?

"This I ask Thee, O Ahura! tell me aright: who fashioned Âramaiti (our piety) the beloved, together with Thy Sovereign Power? Who, through his guiding wisdom, hath made the son revering the father? Who made him beloved?

With questions such as these, so abundant, O Mazda! I press Thee, O beautiful Spirit, Thou maker of all!

"This I ask Thee, O Ahura! tell me aright, that I may ponder these which are Thy revelations, O Mazda! and the words which were asked of Thee by Thy Good Mind Within us, and that whereby we may attain, through Thine Order, to this life's perfection. Yea, how may my soul with joyfulness increase in goodness?

. . . . .

"This I ask Thee, O Ahura! tell me aright that holy faith which is of all Things best, and which, going on hand in hand with Thy people, shall further my lands in Asha, Thine Order, and, through the words of Âramaiti (our piety), shall render actions just. The prayers of mine understanding will seek for Thee, O Ahura!

. . . . .

"This I ask Thee, O Ahura! tell me aright: who is the righteous one in that regard in which I ask Thee my question? And who is evil? For which is the wicked? Or which is himself the foremost wicked one? And the vile man who stands against me in this gain of Thy blessing, wherefore is he not held and believed to be the sinner that he is?

This I ask Thee, O Ahura! tell me aright: how shall I banish this Demon-of-the-Lie from us hence to those beneath who are filled with rebellion?"

CONFESSION OF FAITH

"The good, righteous, right religion which the Lord has sent to the creatures is that which Zarathustra has brought. The religion is the religion of Zarathustra, the religion of Ahura-Mazda, given to Zarathustra."

THE CREED[9]

"I praise the well-thought, well-spoken, well-performed thoughts, words, and works.

"I lay hold on all good thoughts, words, and works.

"I abandon all evil thoughts, words, and works. I bring to you, O Aměsha-çpěntas,

"Praise and adoration,

"With thoughts, words, and works, with heavenly mind, the vital strength of my own body.

. . . . .

"I drive away the Daêvas, I profess myself a Zarathrustrian, an expeller of the Daêvas, a follower of the teachings of Ahura.

"A hymn-singer of the Aměsha-çpěntas, a praiser of the Aměsha-çpěntas.

"To Ahura-Mazda, the good, endued with good wisdom, I offer all good."

PRAYER OF KEM NÂ MAZDA [10]

"Whom hast thou placed to protect me, O Mazda, while the hate of the fiend is grasping me? Whom but thy Atar and Vohumanô (*Angels in charge of Heaven*), by whose work the holy world goes on?

"Reveal to me the rules of thy law!"

PRAYER OF KE VERETHREM GA

"Who is he who will smite the fiend in order to maintain thy ordinances? Teach me clearly thy rules for this world and for the next, that Shros (*Angel who fights Drug with an uplifted Club, and guards the Earth Night and Day*) may come with Vohumanô and help whomsoever thou pleasest."

PRAYER OF ORMUZD YAST
(In Praise of God)

. . . . .

"And he who in this material world, O Spitama Zarathustra! shall recite and pronounce those names of mine either by day or by night;

"He who shall pronounce them, when he rises up or when he lays him down; . . . when he binds on the sacred girdle or when he unbinds the sacred girdle; when he goes out of his dwelling-place, or when he goes out of his town, or when he goes out of his country and comes into another country;

"That man, neither in that day nor in that night, shall be wounded by the weapons of the foe who rushes with anger and is Drug-minded;

. . . . .

"But those names shall come in to keep him from behind and to keep him in front, from the Drug unseen, . . . from the evil-doer bent on mischief, and from that fiend who is all death, Angro Mainyus."

GOD AS THE KING, THE LIFE, THE REWARDER[11]

"Praises, and songs, and adorations do we offer to Ahura-Mazda, and to Righteousness the Best; yea, we offer and we ascribe them, and proclaim them.

"And to Thy good kingdom, O Ahura-Mazda! may we attain for ever, and a good King be Thou over us; and let each man of us, and so each woman, thus abide, O Thou most beneficent of beings, and for both the worlds!

. . . . .

"So mayst Thou be to us our life, and our body's vigour, O Thou most beneficent of beings, and that for both the worlds!

"Aye, let us win and conquer long life, O Ahura-Mazda! in Thy grace, and through Thy will may we be powerful. Mayst Thou lay hold on us to help, . . . and with salvation, O Thou most beneficent of beings!

. . . . .

"What reward most meet for our deserving Thou hast appointed for the souls, O Ahura-Mazda! of that do Thou bestow on us for this life, and for that of mind. Of that reward do Thou Thyself grant this advantage, that we may come under Thy protecting guardianship, and that of Righteousness for ever."

. . . . .

THE CREATION OF THE WORLD BY AHURA-MAZDA AND CORRESPONDING EVILS BY ANGRO MAINYUS [12]

Ahura-Mazda spake unto Spitama Zarathustra, saying:
"I have made every land dear to its dwellers, even though it had no charms whatever in it. Had I not made every land dear to its dwellers, even though it had no charms whatever in it, then the whole living world would have invaded the Airyana Vaêgô."

Countries and Lands Created by Ahura-Mazda.

1. *Airyana Vaêgô by the good river Dâitya.*
2. *The plains of Sughdha.*
3. *The land of Mourn (Merv).*
4. *Bâkhdhi with high-lifted banners (Balkh).*
5. *The land of Nisâya.*
6. *Harôyu with its lakes (Herat).*
7. *Vaêkereta (Cabul).*
8. *Urva of the rich pastures (land in Khorasan).*

9. Khnenta in Vehrkâna.
10. Harahvaiti the beautiful.
11. The bright and glorious Haêtumant.
12. Ragha of the three races (Rai, the birthplace of Zoroaster).
13. Holy Kakhra.
14. The four-cornered Varena.
15. Country of the Seven Rivers.
16. The land by the floods of the Rangha.

Corresponding Evils Placed there by Angro Mainyus (The Evil Spirit).

1. The serpent and winter.
2. The fly Skaitya, which stings and brings death to the cattle.
3. Sinful lusts.
4. Corn-eating ants.
5. The sin of unbelief.
6. The stained mosquito.
7. The Pairika Knāthaiti (meaning an evil creature or a pari who destroys mankind)
8. The sin of pride and tyranny.
9. Unnatural sin.
10. Sin of defiling the virgin earth by burying corpses.
11. Witchcraft and wizards.
12. Sin of utter unbelief (atheism).
13. Sin of burning of corpses.
14. Illness of women.
15. Excessive heat.
16. Excessive frost.

"There are still other lands and countries, beautiful and deep, desirable and bright and thriving."

GOD'S WARNING TO YIMA
OF WINTER AND DELUGE [13]

And Ahura-Mazda spake unto Yima, saying:
"O fair Yima, son of Vîvanghat! upon the material world the

fatal winters are going to fall, that shall bring the fierce, foul frost; . . . that shall make snow-flakes fall thick, even an *aredvî*, deep on the highest tops of mountains.

"And all the three sorts of beasts shall perish, those that live in the wilderness, and those that live on the tops of the mountains, and those that live in the bosom of the dale, under the shelter of stables.

"Therefore make thee a *vara*, [14] long as a riding-ground on every side of the square, and thither bring . . . sheep and oxen . . . men . . . dogs . . . birds and . . . red blazing fires.

. . . . . .

"There thou shalt make waters flow in a bed a *hâthra* [15] long; there thou shalt settle birds, by the ever-green banks that bear never-failing food. There thou shalt establish dwelling-places, consisting of a house with a balcony, a courtyard, and a gallery.

"Thither thou shalt bring . . . men and women, of the greatest, best, and finest kinds on this earth; thither thou shalt bring . . . every kind of cattle, of the greatest, best, and finest kinds on this earth. Thither thou shalt bring the seeds of every kind of fruit, the fullest of food and sweetest of odour. All those . . . shalt thou bring, two of every kind, to be kept inexhaustible there, so long as those men shall stay in the vara.

"There shall be no hump-backed, none bulged forward there; no impotent, no lunatic, no poverty, no lying, no meanness, no jealousy, no decayed tooth, no leprous to be confined, nor any of the brands wherewith Angro Mainyus stamps the bodies of mortals."

Then Yima said within himself: "How shall I manage to make that vara which Ahura-Mazda has commanded me to make?"

And Ahura-Mazda said unto Yima: ". . .

Crush the earth with a stamp of thy heel, and then knead it with thy hands . . ."

BLESSINGS OF CULTIVATING THE SOIL [16]

"He who would till the earth, . . . with the left arm and the right, . . . unto him will she bring forth plenty, like a loving bride, on her bed, unto her beloved; the bride will bring forth children, the earth will bring forth plenty of fruit.

"He who sows corn sows holiness: he makes the law of Mazda grow higher and higher.

. . . . . .

"When barley is coming forth, the Daêvas start up; when corn is growing *ripe*, then faint the Daêvas' hearts; when the corn is being ground, the Daêvas groan; when wheat is coming forth, the Daêvas are destroyed. In that house they can no longer stay; from that house they are beaten away, wherein wheat is thus coming forth.

. . . . .

"He who tilling the earth, . . . would not kindly and piously give to one of the faithful, he shall fall down into the darkness . . . down into the world of woe, the dismal realm, down into the house of hell."

HAPPINESS OF THE EARTH [17]

"It is the place whereon one of the faithful erects a house with a priest within, with cattle, with a wife, with children, and good herds within; and wherein afterwards the cattle go on thriving, holiness is thriving, fodder is thriving, the dog is thriving, the wife is thriving, the child is thriving, the fire is thriving, and every blessing of life is thriving.

. . . . .

"It is the place where one of the faithful cultivates most corn, grass, and fruit; . . . where he waters ground that is dry, or dries ground that is too wet.

"It is the place where there is most increase of flocks and herds."

GRIEF OF THE EARTH [18]

. . . . .

"It is the place wherein most corpses of dogs and of men lie buried.

. . . . .

"It is the place whereon the wife and children of one of the faithful . . . are driven along the way of captivity (the dry, the dusty way, and lift up a voice of wailing.

"Unhappy is the land that has long lain unsown with the seed of the sower, and wants a good husbandman, like a well-shapen maiden who has long gone childless and wants a good husband."

. . . . .

CULTIVATION OF LAND
WHERE A CORPSE IS FOUND [19]

". . . A year long shall the ground lie fallow whereon dogs or men have died."

PURIFICATION OF WATER
DEFILED BY A CORPSE [20]

"O Maker of the material world, thou Holy One! if a worshipper of Mazda, walking, or running, or riding, or driving, come upon a corpse in a stream of running water, what shall he do?"

Ahura-Mazda answered: "Taking off his shoes, putting off his clothes, boldly, O Zarathustra! he shall enter the river, and take the dead out of the water. . . .

"He shall draw out of the water as much of the corpse as he can. . . . No sin attaches to him for any bone, hair . . . that may drop back into the water.

. . . . .

"As long as the corpse has not been taken out of the water, so long shall that water be unclean and unfit to drink.

"After the corpse has been taken out and the stream has flowed three times,[21] the water is clean. . . ."

RELIGIOUS EDUCATION [22]

"He shall learn on during the first part of the day and the last, during the first part of the night and the last, that his mind may be increased in knowledge and wax strong in holiness: so shall he sit up, giving thanks and praying to God and *His angels* that he may be increased in knowledge. He shall rest during the middle part of the day, during the middle part of the night, and thus shall he continue until he can say ail the words which former Athrapaitis[23] have said."

REWARD FOR THE PIOUS [24]

Zarathustra asked Ahura-Mazda: "O thou all-knowing Ahura-Mazda, should I urge upon the godly man, should I urge upon the godly woman, should I urge upon the wicked Daêva-worshipper who lives in sin, that they have once to leave behind them the earth made by Ahura, that they have to leave the water that runs, the corn that grows, and all the rest of their wealth?"

Ahura-Mazda answered: "Thou shouldst, O holy Zarathustra."

"O Maker of the material world, thou Holy One! where are the rewards given? Where does the rewarding take place? Where is the rewarding fulfilled? Whereto do men come to take the reward that, in their life in the material world, they have won for their souls?"

Ahura-Mazda answered: "When the man is dead, when his time is over, then the hellish, evil-doing Daêvas assail him; and when the third night is gone, when the dawn appears and brightens up, and makes Mithra[25] . . . reach the all-happy mountains, and the sun is rising:

Then the fiend named Vîzaresha carries off in bonds the souls of the wicked Daêva-worshippers who live in sin. The soul enters the way made by Time, and open both to the wicked and to the righteous. At the head of the Kinvad (*chinvat*) Bridge . . . they ask for their spirits and souls the reward for the worldly goods which they gave away here below.

. . . . .

"Up rises Vohumanô (Door-Keeper of Heaven) from his golden seat. Vohumanô exclaims: 'How hast thou come to us, thou Holy One, from that decaying world into this undecaying one?'

"Gladly pass the souls of the righteous to the golden seat of Ahura-Mazda, to the golden seat of the Ameshaspentas, [26] to Garodemana.[27]"

FORGIVENESS OF SIN [28]

"The law of Mazda indeed, O Spitama Zarathustra! takes away from him who confesses it the bonds of his sin; it takes away the sin of breach of trust; it takes away the sin of murdering one of the faithful; it takes away the sin of burying a corpse; it takes away the sin of deeds for which there is no atonement; it takes away the heaviest penalties of sin; it takes away any sin that may be sinned."

THE TEMPTATION [29]

Thus Zarathustra answered Angro Mainyus (*the Evil Spirit*): "O evil-doer, Angro Mainyus! I will smite the creation of the Daêva; I will smite the Nasu, a creature of the Daêva. . . ."

Again to him said the guileful one, ... Angro Mainyus: "Do not destroy my creatures, O holy Zarathustra! . . . Renounce the good law of the worshippers of Mazda, and thou shalt gain such a boon as *Zohâk*, the murderer, gained, the ruler of the nations."

Thus in answer to him said Spitama Zarathustra: "No! never will

I renounce the good law of the worshippers of Mazda, though my body, my life, my soul should burst!"

Again to him said the guileful one . . . Angro Mainyus: "By whose word wilt thou strike, by whose word wilt thou repel, by whose weapon will the good creatures strike and repel my creation?" . . .

". . . The words taught by Mazda, these are my . . . best weapons! By this word will I strike, by this word will I repel . . . O evil-doer, Angro Mainyus! To me Spenta Mainyus (Good Spirit) gave it; he gave it to me in the boundless time; to me the Ameshaspentas (*Archangels*), the all-ruling, the all-beneficent, gave it."

Zarathustra chanted aloud the (*prayer of*) AHUNA VAIRYA.

"The will of the Lord is the law of holiness. The riches of Vohumanô (*Good Mind*) shall be given to him who works in this world for Mazda, and wields according to the will of Ahura the power he gave to him to relieve the poor." . . . . . . They run away, the wicked, evil-doing Daêvas; they run away, casting the evil eye, the wicked, evil-doing Daêvas.

"'Let us gather together at the head of Arezûra (*the Gate of Hell*). For he is . . . born, the holy Zarathustra, in the house of Pourushaspa. How can we procure his death? He is the stroke that fells the fiends.' . . .

"Down are the Daêva-worshippers, the Nasu made by the Daêva, the false-speaking lie! They run away, they rush away, the wicked, evil-doing Daêvas, into the depths of the dark, horrid world of hell."

BANISHMENT OF ANGRO MAINYUS

"Away art thou driven, O mischievous Angro Mainyus! from the fire, from the water, from the earth, from the cow, from the tree, from the faithful man, and from the faithful woman . . . from all good things made by Mazda, the offspring of the holy principle."

ON LOAN[30]

He who does not restore (a thing lent) when it is asked for back again, steals the thing; he robs the man. So he does every day, every night, as long as he keeps in his house his neighbour's property, as though it were his own."

ON WASTE [31]

"Ahura-Mazda, indeed, does not allow us to waste anything of value that we may have, not even so much as an Asperena's weight of thread, not even so much as a maid lets fall in spinning."

TEMPERANCE [32]

"Regarding wine, it is evident that it is possible for good and bad temper to come to manifestation through wine.

. . . . .

"It is not requisite for investigation, because he who is a good-tempered man, when he drinks wine, is such-like as a gold or silver cup which, however much more they burn it, becomes purer and brighter. It also keeps his thoughts, words, and deeds more virtuous; and he becomes gentler and pleasanter unto wife and child, companions and friends, and is more diligent in every duty and good work.

"And he who is a bad-tempered man, when he drinks wine, thinks and considers himself more than ordinary: He carries on a quarrel with companions, displays insolence, makes ridicule and mockery, and acts arrogantly to a good person. He distresses his own wife and child, slave and servant; and dissipates the joy of the good, carries off peace, and brings in discord.

"But every one must be cautious as to the moderate drinking of wine. Because, from the moderate drinking of wine, thus much benefit happens to him: since it digests the food, kindles the vital fire, increases the understanding and intellect, and blood, removes vexation, and inflames the complexion.

It causes recollection of things forgotten, and goodness takes a place in the mind. It likewise increases the sight of the eye, the hearing of the ear, and the speaking of the tongue; and work, which it is necessary to do and expedite, becomes more progressive. He also sleeps pleasantly and rises light.

"And in him who drinks wine more than moderately, . . . himself, wife, and child, friend and kindred, are distressed and unhappy, and the superintendent of troubles and the enemy are glad. The sacred beings, also, are not pleased with him; and infamy comes to his body, and even wickedness to his soul.

"And even he who gives wine authorizedly unto any one, and he is thereby intoxicated by it, is equally guilty of every sin which that drunkard commits owing to that drunkenness." [33]

SOULS' VISIT TO THE EARTH [34]

We worship the good, strong, beneficent Fravashis [35] of the faithful, who come and go through the borough at the time of the Hamaspathmaêdha [36]; they go along there for ten nights, asking thus:

"Who will praise us? Who will offer us a sacrifice? Who will meditate upon us? Who will bless us? Who will receive us with meat and clothes in his hand and with a prayer worthy of bliss? Of which of us will the name be taken for invocation? Of which of you will the soul be worshipped by you with a sacrifice? To whom will the gift of ours be given, that he may have never-failing food for ever and ever?" And the man who offers them up a sacrifice, with meat and clothes in his hand, with a prayer worthy of bliss, the awful [37] Fravashis of the faithful, satisfied, unharmed, and unoffended, bless thus:

"May there be in this house flocks of animals and men! May there be a swift horse and a solid chariot! May there be a man who knows how to praise God and rule in an assembly, who will offer us sacrifices with meat and clothes in his hand, and with a prayer worthy of bliss!"

THE MAZDAYASNIAN CONFESSION [38]

"I drive the Daêvas hence; I confess as a Mazda-worshipper of the order of Zarathustra, estranged from the Daêvas, devoted to the lore of the Lord, a praiser of the Bountiful Immortals; and to Ahura-Mazda, the good and endowed with good possessions, I attribute all things good, to the Holy One, the resplendent, to the glorious, whose are all things whatsoever which are good; whose is the Kine, whose is Asha (the righteous order pervading all things pure), whose are the stars, in whose lights the glorious beings and objects are clothed.

"And I choose Piety, the bounteous and the good, mine may she be! And therefore I loudly deprecate all robbery and violence against the (Sacred) Kine, and all drought to the wasting of the Mazdayasnian villages.

. . . . . .

"Never may I stand as a source of wasting, never as a source of withering to the Mazdayasnian villages, not for the love of body or of life.

"Away do I abjure the shelter and headship of the Daêvas, evil as they are; aye, utterly bereft of good, and void of virtue, deceitful in their wickedness, of all beings those most like the Demon-of-the-Lie, the most loathsome of existing things, and the ones the most of all bereft of good.

"Off, off, do I abjure the Daêvas and all possessed by them, the sorcerers and all that hold to their devices, and every existing being of the sort; their thoughts do I abjure, their words and actions, and their seed that propagate their sin; away do I abjure their shelter and their headship.

"Thus and so in every deed might Ahura-Mazda have indicated to Zarathustra in every question which Zarathustra asked, and in all the consultations in the which they two conversed together. Thus and so might Zarathustra have abjured the shelter and the headship of the Daêvas in all the questions and in all the consultations with which they two conversed together, Zarathustra and the Lord.

"And so I myself, in whatsoever circumstances I may be placed, as a worshipper of Mazda, and of Zarathustra's order, would so abjure the Daêvas and their shelter, as he who was the holy Zarathustra abjured them.

"To that religious sanctity to which the waters appertain, do I belong, to that sanctity to which the plants, to that sanctity to which the Kine of blessed gift, to that religious sanctity to which Ahura-Mazda, who made both Kine and holy men, belongs, to that sanctity do I.

"A Mazda-worshipper I am, of Zarathustra's order; so do I confess, as a praiser and confessor, and I therefore praise aloud the well-thought thought, the word well spoken, and the deed well done.

"Yea, I praise at once the Faith of Mazda, the Faith which has no faltering utterance, the Faith that wields the felling halbert, the holy (Creed), which is the most imposing, best, and most beautiful of all religions which exist, and of all that shall in future come to knowledge, Ahura's Faith, the Zarathustrian creed. Yea, to Ahura-Mazda do I ascribe all good, and such shall be the worship of the Mazdayasnian belief!"

PATET ERANI [39]
Prayer for Repentance

"I am wholly without doubt in the existence of the good Mazdayasnian faith, in the coming of the resurrection and the later body, in the stepping over the bridge Chinvat, in an invariable recompense of good deeds and their reward, and of bad deeds and their punishment, as well as in the continuance of Paradise, in the annihilation of Hell and Ahriman [40] and the Daêvas, that [God] Ahura-Mazda will at last be victorious and Ahriman will perish together with the Daêvas and the off-shoots of darkness.

. . . . .

"All that I ought to have thought and have not thought, all that I ought 'to have said and have not said, all that I ought to have done and have not done, all that I ought to have ordered and have not ordered, all that I ought not to have thought and yet have thought, all that I ought not to have spoken and yet have spoken, all that I ought not to have done and yet have done, all that I ought not to have ordered and yet have ordered; for thoughts, words, and works, bodily and spiritual, earthy and heavenly, pray I for forgiveness, and repent of it with Patet. [41]

. . . . .

"This heavenly Patet shall be a fast brazen wall . . . that it may keep the gate of Hell fast in bonds, and the way to Paradise open, the way to that best place:—to the shining Garothman which possesses all majesty, that our soul and the souls of the pure at the Bridge Chinvat, the great, may step over freed from trouble and easily, and may the pure Srosh, [42] the victorious, friend, protector, overseer, be the protector and the watcher of my soul. . . ."

MARRIAGE SERVICE [43]

"Do you both accept the contract for life with honourable mind, that pleasure may increase to ye twain?

Admonitions

"In the name and friendship of Ahura-Mazda. Be ever shining . . . Be increasing! Be victorious! Learn purity! Be worthy of good praise! May the mind think good thoughts, the words speak good, the works do good! . . . Be a Mazdayasnian, accomplish works according to thy mind . . . speak truth . . . and be obedient. Be modest with friends, clever, and well-wishing. Be not cruel. Be not wrathful-minded. Commit no sin through shame. Be not covetous. Torment not. Cherish not wicked envy, be not haughty, treat no one despitefully, cherish no lust. Rob not the property of others, keep thyself from the wives of others. Do good works with good activity. . . . Enter into no strife with a revengeful man. Be no companion to a covetous one. Go not on the same way with a cruel one. Enter into no agreement with one of ill-fame. . . . Combat the adversaries with right. . . . Enter into no strife with those of evil repute. Before an assembly speak only pure words. Before kings speak with moderation. In no wise displease thy mother. Keep thine own body pure in justice.

. . . . .

Blessings

"May Ahura-Mazda (God) send you gifts, Bahman, thinking with the soul; Ardibihist good speech; Sharevar, good working; Çependarmat, wisdom; Khordat, sweetness and prosperity; Amertat, fruitfulness!

"May that come to you which is better than the good, may that not come to you which is worse than the evil. . . ."

THE VISION OF ARDÂ-VIRÂF [44]

They say that, once upon a time, the pious Zaratûtsht (Zoroaster) made the religion which he had received current in the world; and till the completion of three hundred years the religion was in purity, and men were without doubts.

. . . . .

And this religion, namely all the Avesta and Zend, written upon prepared cow-skins and with gold ink, was deposited in the archives in Stâkhar Pâpâkân; and the hostility of the evil-destined, wicked Ashemôk, the evil-doer, brought onward Alexander, the Rûman who was dwelling in Egypt, and he burnt them up.

. . . . .

And after that there was confusion and contention among the people of the country of Iran, one with the other.

. . . . .

And afterwards there were other magi and Desturs [45] of the religion, and some of their number were loyal and apprehensive. And an assembly of them was summoned in the residence of the victorious Frôbâg fire; and there were speeches and good ideas of many kinds on this subject: that "it is necessary for us to seek a means so that some of us may go and bring intelligence from the spirits; that the people who exist in this age shall know whether these Yazashni and Drôn and Afrînagân ceremonies, and Nîran prayers, and ablutions and purifications which we bring into operation attain unto God or unto the demons, and come to the relief of our souls or not.

. . . . .

And from the seven, three were selected, and from the three, one only, named Vîrâf, and some called him the Nîshâpûrian. Then that Vîrâf, as he heard that decision, stood upon his feet, joined his hands on his breast, and spake thus, "If it please you, then give me not the undesired narcotic till you cast lots for the Mazdayasnians and me; and if the lot come to me, I shall go willingly to that place of the pious and the wicked, and carry this message correctly, and bring an answer truly.

. . . . .

"After I had drunk the consecrated wine, and I had reposed my body to rest, and given my mind up to the adoration of God, methought my soul took its flight towards the holy regions, where Serosh Izad [46] appeared unto me, and beckoned me towards him, when, after giving and receiving the customary salutations, Serosh Izad said to me, 'You have made a long journey in the faith. I am happy to see you in these blessed regions, and your escape from the world of wickedness gives one great pleasure; but, Ardâ-Vîrâf, you have come before your time. What is the occasion?' Ardâ-Vîrâf replied in accents of complacency, 'I have been sent, O Serosh Izad! by the king, by the priests, and by the voice of the nation in general, on this embassy, to know of heaven and hell, in order that heresy and schism be banished from the earth, and that the worship of the true God be restored to its wonted purity.'

. . . . .

". . . On saying this, Serosh Izad took hold of me by the arm, and led me forward across the bridge, when the throne of Mehr Izad, [47] came in view, with Roshni Izad [48] standing by him, holding in his hands the scales of justice, made of pure gold, and having on his right hand and on his left five thousand angels, and whose different petitions he can hear at once, and if written can see at one glance. Having saluted, and having my salutation returned, the attending angels surrounded me, and thus addressed me, 'O Ardâ-Virâf! your time has not yet come. How and by what means have you come thus far?' I answered, 'I have come thus far by the assistance of God, at the request of my king, Ardeshir Babegan, of the priests, and of the people, to collect and report the wonders of heaven and hell; that I may see that the truth may by these means be again restored to the earth, and heresy and wickedness banished for ever.'

"... Afterwards arose Vohûmano,[49] the archangel, from a throne made of gold, and he took hold of my hand. With the words 'good thought' and 'good word' and 'good deed,' he brought me into the midst of Aûharmazd [50] and the archangels and other holy ones, and the guardian angels of Zaratûsht Spitâma, Kaî-Vishtâsp, Jâmasp, Isâdvâstar, the son of Zaratûsht, and other upholders and leaders of the religion, than whom I have never seen any one more brilliant and excellent.

"And Vohûman said thus, 'This is Aûharmazd.' And I wished to offer worship before him.

"And he said to me thus, 'Salutation to thee, Ardâ-Vîrâf, thou art welcome; from that perishable world thou hast come to this pure bright place.' And he ordered Srôsh the pious, and Atarô [51] the angel, thus, 'Take Ardâ-Vîrâf, and show him the place and reward of the pious, and also the punishment of the wicked.'

. . . . .

"And I saw the darkest hell, which is pernicious, dreadful, terrible, very painful, mischievous, and evil-smelling. And after further observation it appeared to me as a pit, at the bottom of which a thousand cubits would not reach; and though all the wood which is in the world were put on to the fire in this most stinking and gloomy hell, it would never emit a smell; and again also, as close as the ear to the eye, and as many as the hairs on the mane of a horse, so close and many in number the souls of the wicked stand—but they see not and hear no sound one from the other; every one thinks thus, 'I am alone!' And for them are the gloom of darkness and the stench and fearfulness of the torment and punishment of hell of various kinds; so that whoever is only a day in hell cries out thus, 'Are not those nine thousand years yet completed when they should release us from this hell?'

. . . . .

"'Without trouble nothing can be attained,' said Serosh Izad; 'the poor day-labourer is worthy of his hire, and those who perform good works will have their reward in eternal life, according to their several merits.' He continued, 'The life of man is of short duration, and many troubles and anxieties fall to his lot; and a man, after fifty years of prosperity and happiness, may be, by some unforeseen accident, reduced to sickness and poverty. Many are tried by this criterion, and but few are found worthy. To suffer a day of pain, after fifty years of pleasure, is too much for them, and they complain in bitterness of spirit to the Creator of all good of His injustice and cruelty, without remembering the good they have so long enjoyed or calling to mind the eternity of punishment in reserve for the wicked. Therefore, O Ardâ-Vîrâf! walk yourself in the ways of righteousness, and teach others also to do so. Recollect that your body will return to dust, but your soul, if rich in good works, will mount to immortality, and partake of the happiness you have already witnessed. Take less care of your body and more of your soul; the pains and aches of the body are easily cured, but who can minister to the diseases of the soul? When you set out on a journey in the lower world, you provide yourselves, and take with you money, clothes, provisions, and are prepared against all the exigencies of the road, but what do you provide yourselves with for your last journey of the soul from the lower to the upper world, and whose friendship have you to assist you on the way? Hear, O Ardâ-Vîrâf! and I will describe to you the provisions requisite for the voyage to eternal life.

"'In the first place the friend who will assist you is God; but to attain His friendship you must walk in His ways and place in Him the firmest reliance. The provisions must be faith and hope and the remembrance of your good works. The body, O Aida-Viral! may be likened unto a horse, and the soul to its rider, and the provisions requisite for the support of both are good actions; but as with a feeble rider the horse is ill-managed, so with a feeble horse the rider is but ill accommodated. Care ought to be taken that both are kept in order; so, in a spiritual sense, the soul and body must be kept in order by a succession of good actions. Even in the world the multitude would sneer at a man who took more care of his horse than of himself; for this reason a man ought to take more care of his soul than of his body. God, O Ardâ-Vîrâf! requires only two things of the sons of men: the first, that they should not sin; the next, that they should be grateful of the many blessings He is continually bestowing upon them.

"'Let the world, O Ardâ-Vîrâf! be taught not to set their hearts on the pleasures and vanities of life, as nothing can be carried away with them. You have already seen the rewards given to the good and deserving—how they have been repaid for all their trouble; the poor and the rich, the king and the peasant, here receive honours and distinctions according to their good works. The herdsman and shepherd, you have seen their condition.

"'In youth and in the prime of manhood, when blessed with health and vigour, you suppose that your strength will never fail; that your riches, your lands, your houses, and your honours will remain for ever; that your gardens will be always green and your vineyards fruitful. But, O Ardâ-Vîrâf! teach them not to think so teach them the danger of such a way of thinking: all, all will pass away as a dream!

"'The flowers fade, and give lessons unto man that he is unwilling to profit by. Yea, the world itself will pass away, and nothing will remain but God!

"Therefore, O Ardâ-Vîrâf! turn your thoughts only towards Him. No pleasure but has its concomitant pain roses have thorns, and honours fall into disgrace. It is pleasant to drink wine, but intoxication brings pain, if not disgrace; if you exceed in eating, this also brings its punishment, and you must have a doctor; even if you drink the purest water to excess, it engenders dropsy; therefore let the avoidance of excess in everything be most particularly inculcated—in wine or women, in eating and drinking: though they bring their own punishment in the world by the diseases they engender, yet they encourage the most deadly sins, and the soul so indulging will most assuredly be cut off from heaven. So you see, O Ardâ-Vîrâf! that the indulgence of our passions brings no pleasure of long duration, or impresses any good sentiment on the heart.

"'If after praying to God for offspring, and He has granted your request, into what sea of trouble and anxiety are you plunged! Your son or daughter may grow up in vicious habits, and embitter your days by their undutiful conduct: the one may become a thief, the other a courtezan, and bring disgrace on your old age. The bee that produces honey has also a sting.

"'The world is composed of lust, avarice, and of passions the most ungovernable; if God gives them one thing, even that for which they most desire, they are not satisfied, but are continually craving for more and more, to a hundredfold.

"'Avarice and ambition deprive them of sleep, and prevent them from making a laudable exertion to subdue these dreadful passions, which will plunge them into everlasting misery.

"'A king who has conquered all the surrounding countries sighs because he has no more worlds to subdue. Kai Kâus, after having conquered many countries, aspired to be a king in heaven, and was punished for his presumption by a dreadful fall, which made him sensible of his folly.

"'So you see, O Ardâ-Virâf! that content is the happiest condition of man and the most pleasing to the Creator: and treasure the advice I have given you; and as you return to the lower world, inculcate these precepts, and abide by the laws and walk in the way of truth and holiness, and continue in the worship of the true God.'"

. . . . .

SANCTITY [52]

"I pray with benedictions for a benefit, and for the good, even for the entire creation of the holy and the clean; I beseech them for the generation which is now alive, for that which is just coming into life, and for that which shall be hereafter. And I pray for that sanctity which leads to prosperity, and which has long afforded shelter, which goes on hand in hand with it, which joins it in its walk, and of itself becoming its close companion as it delivers forth its precepts, bearing every form of healing virtue which comes to us in waters, appertains to cattle, or is found in plants, and overwhelming all the harmful malice of the Daêvas, and their servants who might harm this dwelling and its lord, bringing good gifts, and better blessings, given very early, and later gifts, leading to successes, and for a long time giving shelter. And so the greatest, and the best, and most beautiful benefits of sanctity fall likewise to our lot for the sacrifice, homage, propitiation, and the praise of the Bountiful Immortals, for the bringing prosperity to this abode, and for the prosperity of the entire creation of the holy, and the clean, and as for this, so for the opposition of the entire evil creation. . . ."

PRAYER FOR SAFETY [53]

"Keep us from our hater, O Mazda! . . . Perish, O fiendish Drug! Perish, O brood of the fiend! Perish, O world of the fiend! . . . . Perish away to the regions of the north, never more to give unto death the living world of the holy spirit!"

---

1. Sacred Books of the East.
2. Spiegel and Bleeck's translation.
3. Sacred Books of the East. Translation by J. Darmesteter.
4. Dinâ-î Maînôg-î Khirad. Sacred Books of the East. Translated by Dr. West.
5. devil.
6. Spiegel and Bleeck's translation.

7. Dâdîstân-î-Dînîk. Sacred Books of the East. Translated by Dr. West.
8. Sacred Books of the East. Yaçna XLIV. Dr. L. H. Mills' translation.
9. Spiegel and Bleeck's translation.
10. Max Müller's "Sacred Books of the East."
11. Sacred Books of the East. Translation by Dr. L. H. Mills.
12. Max Müller's "Sacred Books of the East."
13. Sacred Books of the East.
14. An enclosure.
15. About an English mile.
16. Sacred Books of the East.
17. Sacred Books of the East.
18. Sacred Books of the East.
19. Sacred Books of the East.
20. Sacred Books of the East.
21. Probably tides.
22. Sacred Books of the East.
23. A teaching priest.
24. Max Müller's "Sacred Books of the East."
25. God of Light.
26. Archangels.
27. Highest Heaven.
28. Max Müller's "Sacred Books of the East."
29. Max Müller's "Sacred Books of the East."
30. Sacred Books of the East.
31. Sacred Books of the East.
32. Dînâ-î Maînôg-î Khirad. Sacred Books of the East. Translated by Dr. West.
33. Dâdîstân-î-Dînîk
34. Sacred Books of the East.
35. Souls.
36. The last ten days of the year.
37. Awe-inspiring.
38. Sacred Books of the East. Translated by Dr. L. H. Mills.
39. Spiegel and Bleeck's translation.
40. The Devil.
41. Penance.
42. The Guardian Angel.
43. Spiegel and Bleeck's translation.
44. Dr. Haug and Dr. West's "Ardâ-Virâf"; J. A. Pope's Revelations of Ardâ-Virâf."
45. Chief priests.
46. The Guardian Angel of Souls.
47. Mithra: The Recording Angel.
48. Angel of Justice.
49. Good Mind.
50. Good.
51. God of Fire : The Angel of Life.
52. Sacred Books of the East. Translated by Dr. L. H. Mills.
53. Max Müller's "Sacred Books of the East."

NOTES

Yima was known in the Shah Nameh [1] as Jamshid. Pride was the cause of his downfall. God conferred favours on him, and, according to the Vendidad, he became a mighty and prosperous king. Being elated by success, he disowned God, and in the words of Firdosi thus expressed himself:

> *"'Behold in me the monarch of the world!*
> *By me all nature speaks, by me the thunder's hurl'd.*
> *For me the demons all their magic spread.'*
> *So vain his soul he knew not what he said.*
> *'This world is mine, no other God I know,*
> *From me alone all excellence can flow.'"*

This act of heresy caused his empire to crumble to pieces, and, mighty as he was, he was taken prisoner by the wicked Zohak and sawn in two between planks.

Zohak according to Firdosi, was a son of an Arabian prince. Early in life he had sold his soul to the Devil. He started his infamous reign by murdering his father. At the time when he conquered Jamshid, the Devil had bestowed on him two serpents, one on each shoulder, who had to be fed with human brains. This curse of the Devil brought terrible ruins to the soil of ancient Iran. According to the old Persian legend, Zohak was chained up in a cave on Mount

Demavend by Feridoon, who conquered and ascended the throne of Iran. Zohak is destined to remain there, a prey to anguish, till the day of judgment. Night and day he licks his iron fetters so as to thin the metal and break his bonds. A cock, placed there by the Guardian Angel, gives forth his clarion notes on the break of day, and the fetters of Zohak, rendered thin by hours of licking, with a clang and clatter immediately resume their original size. Thus once more the labour of Zohak has to be begun again. This will go on till the final trumpet call. It is the punishment to one who, in his early folly, sold his soul to the Evil One.

Gāo was a blacksmith during the reign of Zohak. His son was captured by Zohak's retainers, and was destined to feed the serpents with his brains. Gāo, in his terrible anguish to save his child such a horrible and atrocious death, tore off his leathern apron, and, waving it aloft, raised a cry for freedom from his tyrant. The band of soldiers gathered around him under Feridoon, the conqueror of Zohak and liberator of Iran, adopted his apron as the royal standard, which was handed down from generations of rulers of ancient Iran bedecked with precious stones and which was carried aloft in the forefront of numerous battles of historical renown as "Gaviani Zoondo." It proudly floated and shared all the glories of the Persian Empire and veneration of its doughty warriors.

---

1. History of Persian kings, by the great epic poet Firdosi.

Copyright © 2020 by FV Éditions
Cover design : FVE
Hardcover Isbn : 979-10-299-0816-3
All rights reserved.

www.ingramcontent.com/pod-product-compliance
Lightning Source LLC
LaVergne TN
LVHW092232080526
838199LV00104B/101